MY EARS ARE SPECIAL

THE SCIENCE OF SOUND

Physics Book for Children
Children's Physics Books

BABY PROFESSOR

EDUCATION KIDS

Speedy Publishing LLC

40 E. Main St. #1156

Newark, DE 19711

www.speedypublishing.com

Copyright 2017

Have you ever wondered why you have two ears, and how we are able to hear? What exactly is sound and how does it work? In this book, you will discover the answers to these questions and more!

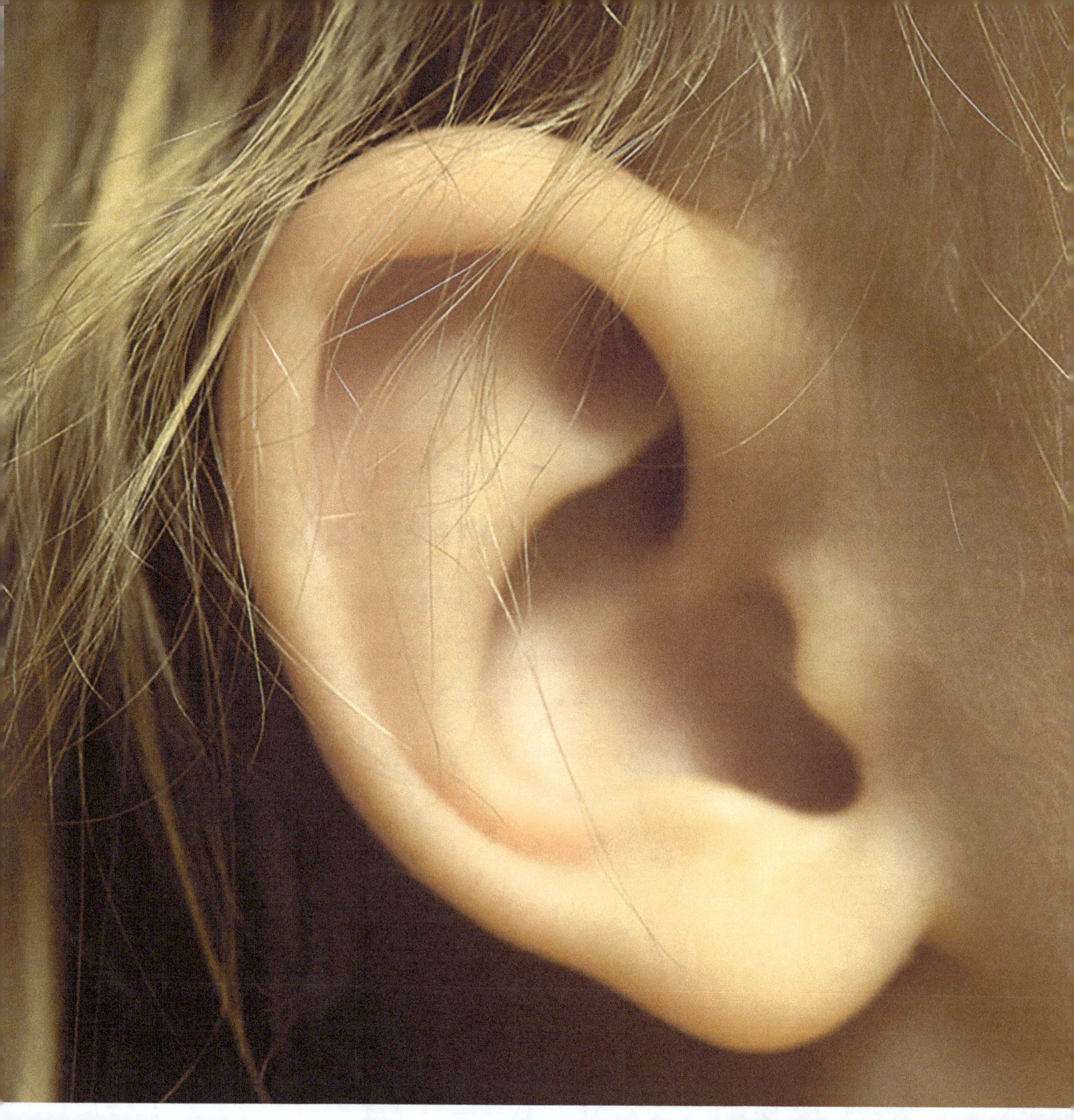

OUR EARS

How we perceive sound is by hearing it. It allows our ears to take the sound waves and create something that can be easily understood by our brain.

The ear consists of the following three major parts:

The outer ear - The outer ear consists of three different sections:

⊃ **The auricle or pinna:** this is what we see on the sides of our head. The part we typically think of when we mention the ear. Its function is to gather the sound and vibrations producing additional sounds.

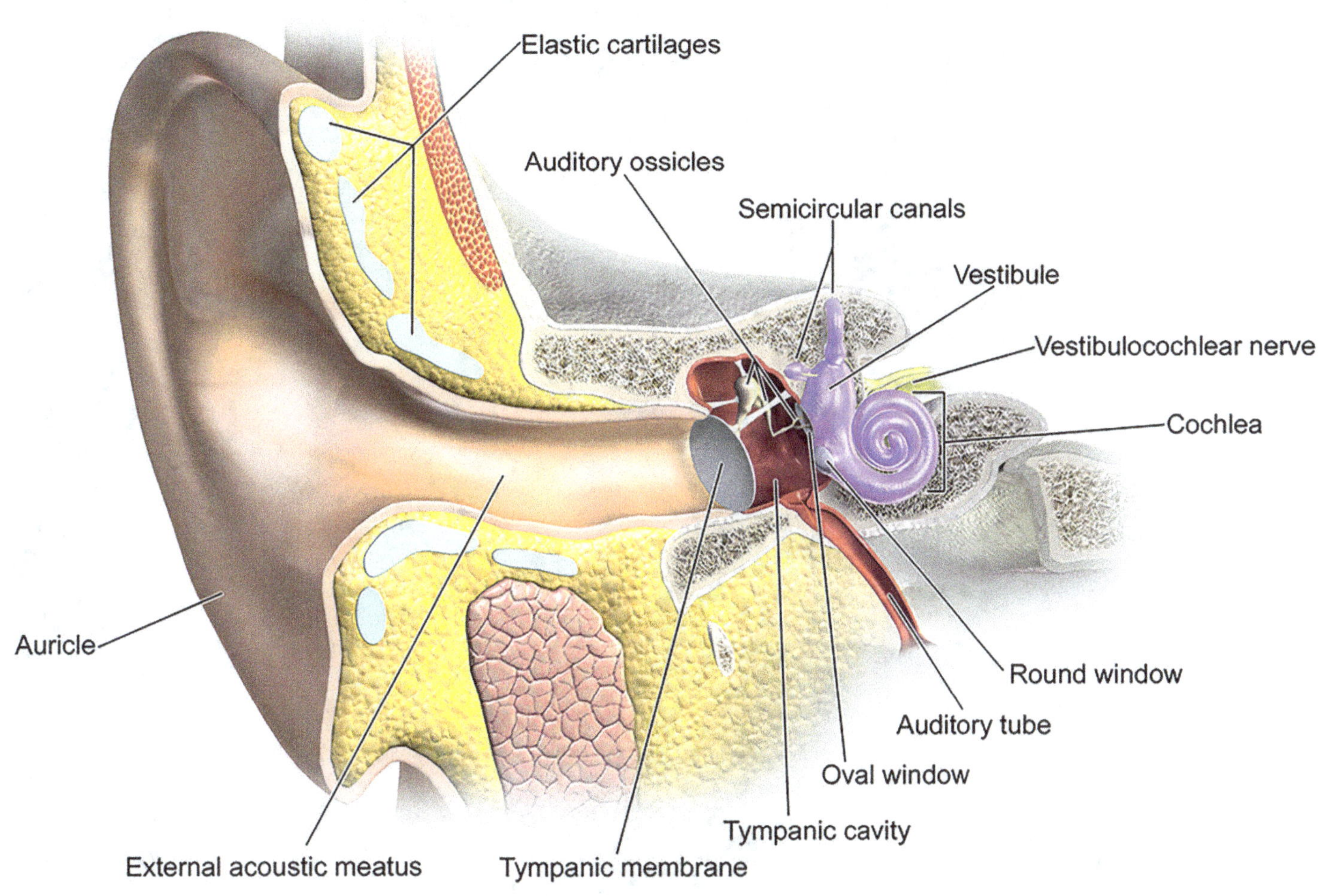

ANATOMY OF THE EAR

- **The ear canal:** This refers to the tube that helps it to travel further into our ear and to get to the next phase of hearing.

- **The eardrum:** This refers to the thin sheet that vibrates as sound reaches it. It is very fragile and sensitive

➲ **It's never a good idea to put anything in your ear, even an item that seems soft and safe can damage it. Have you ever heard the phrase "Don't put anything in your ear smaller than your elbow!"?**

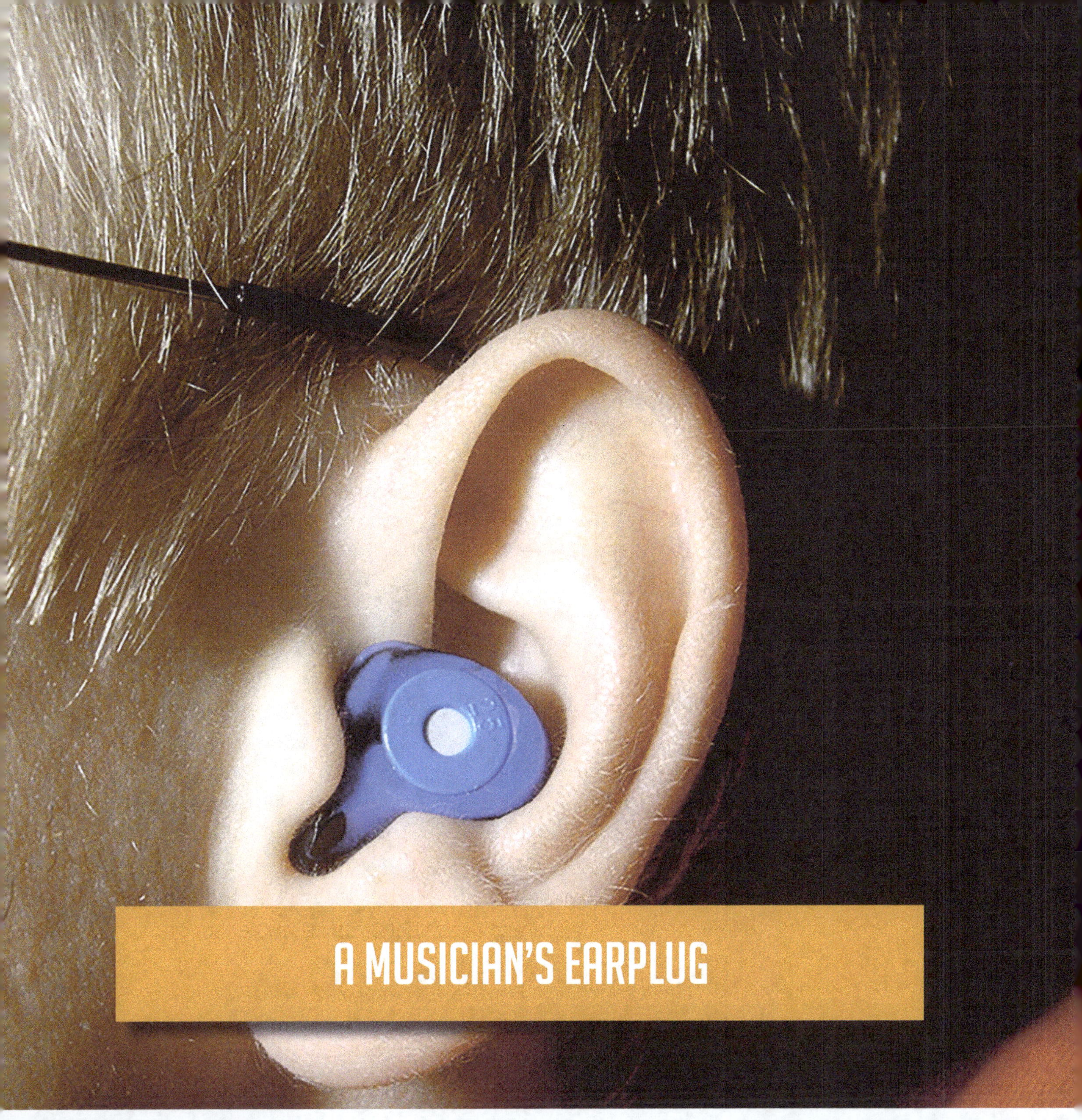

A MUSICIAN'S EARPLUG

The Middle Ear

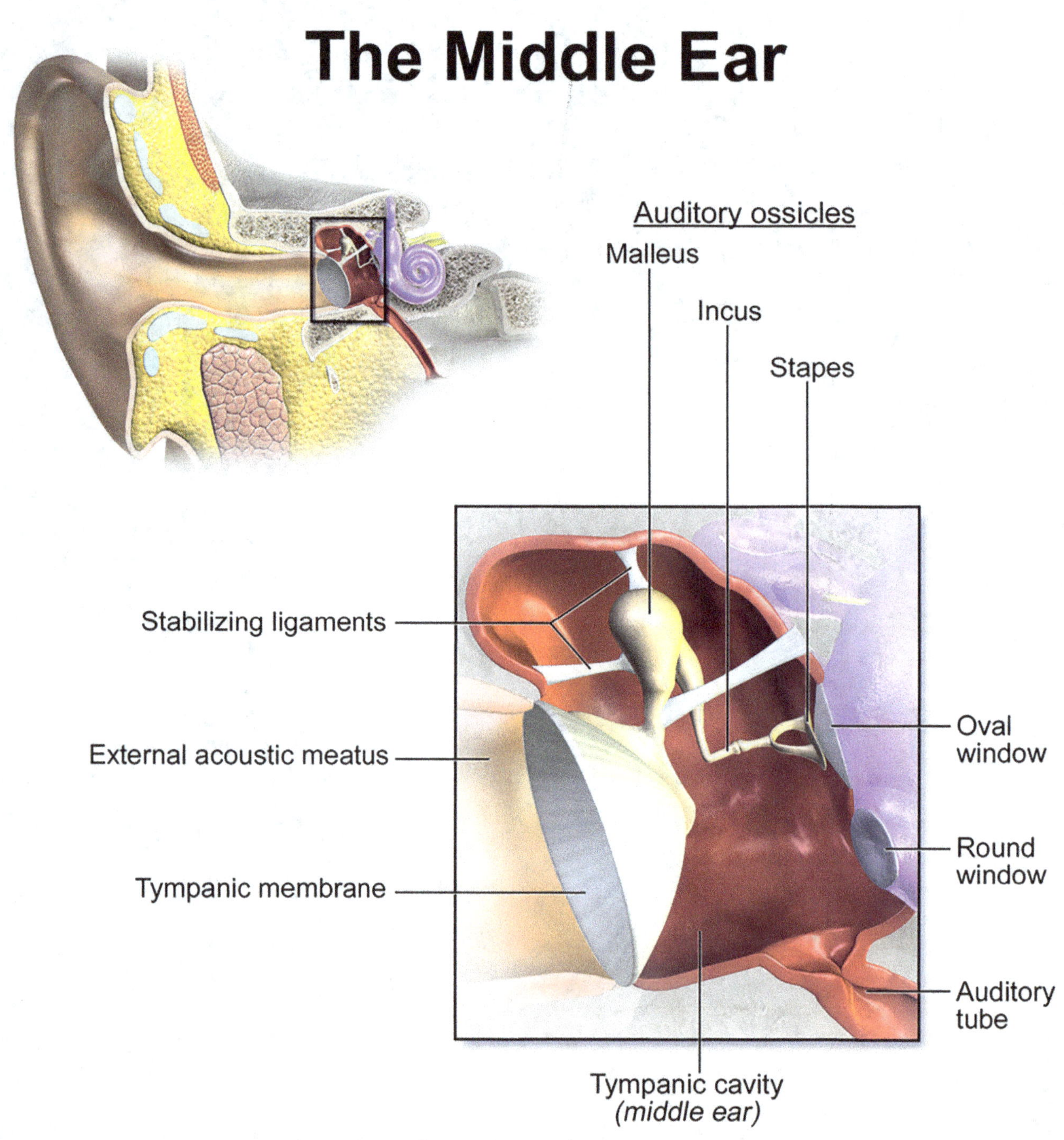

The middle ear – This part of the ear is mostly filled up with air and contains three small bones called **ossicles**. They are named the anvil (incus), hammer (malleus), and the stirrup (stapes). They help to make it louder by amplifying it. The middle ear assists in transferring it to fluid inside the inner ear, which is the next stage. The stirrup is our body's smallest bone.

The inner ear - The inner ear contains fluid and is where the cochlea, or the hearing organ, is located. The cochlea takes the vibrations and translates them to electrical signals so that the nerve can then send it to your brain.

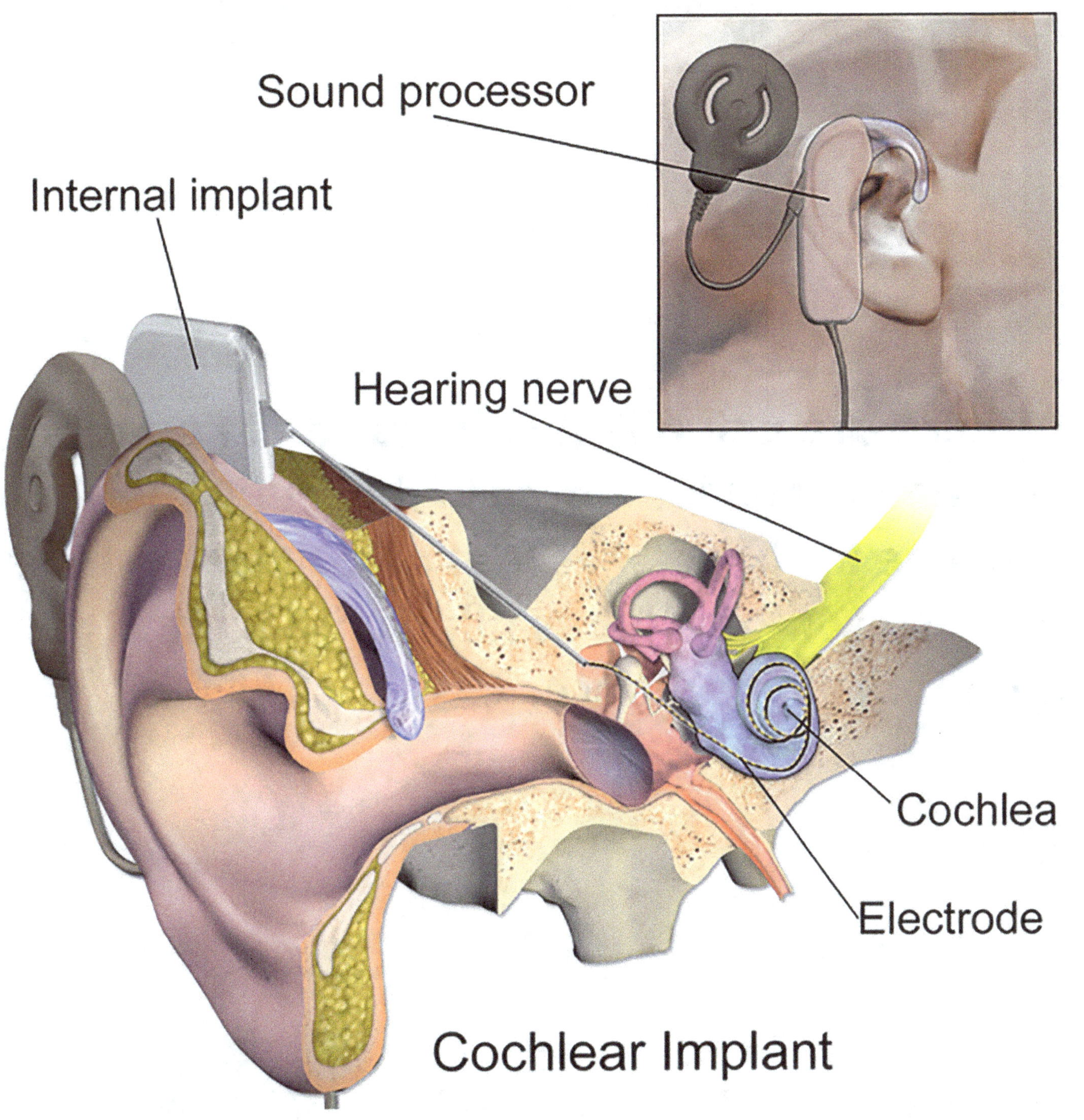

Sound processor
Internal implant
Hearing nerve
Cochlea
Electrode
Cochlear Implant

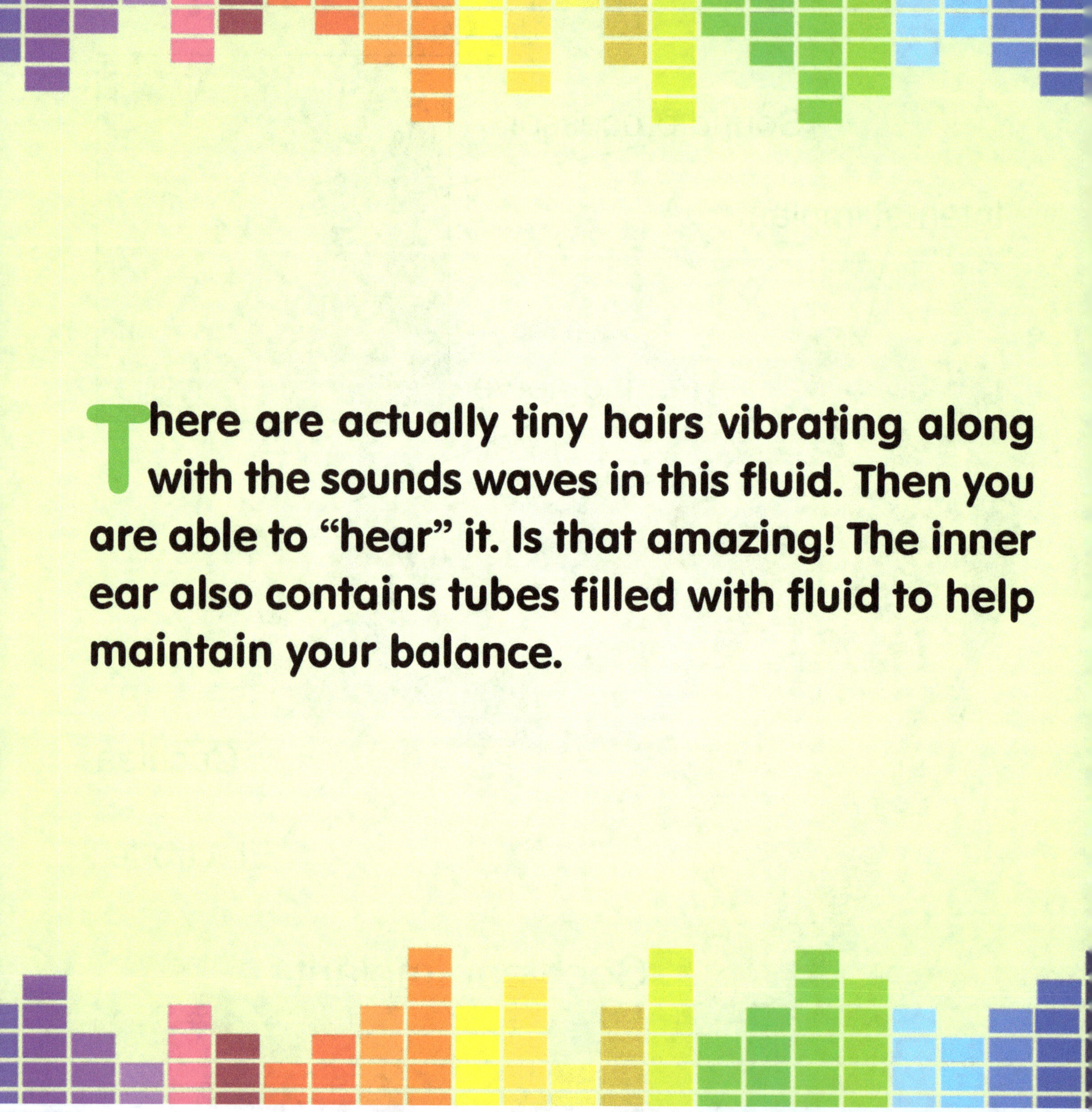

There are actually tiny hairs vibrating along with the sounds waves in this fluid. Then you are able to "hear" it. Is that amazing! The inner ear also contains tubes filled with fluid to help maintain your balance.

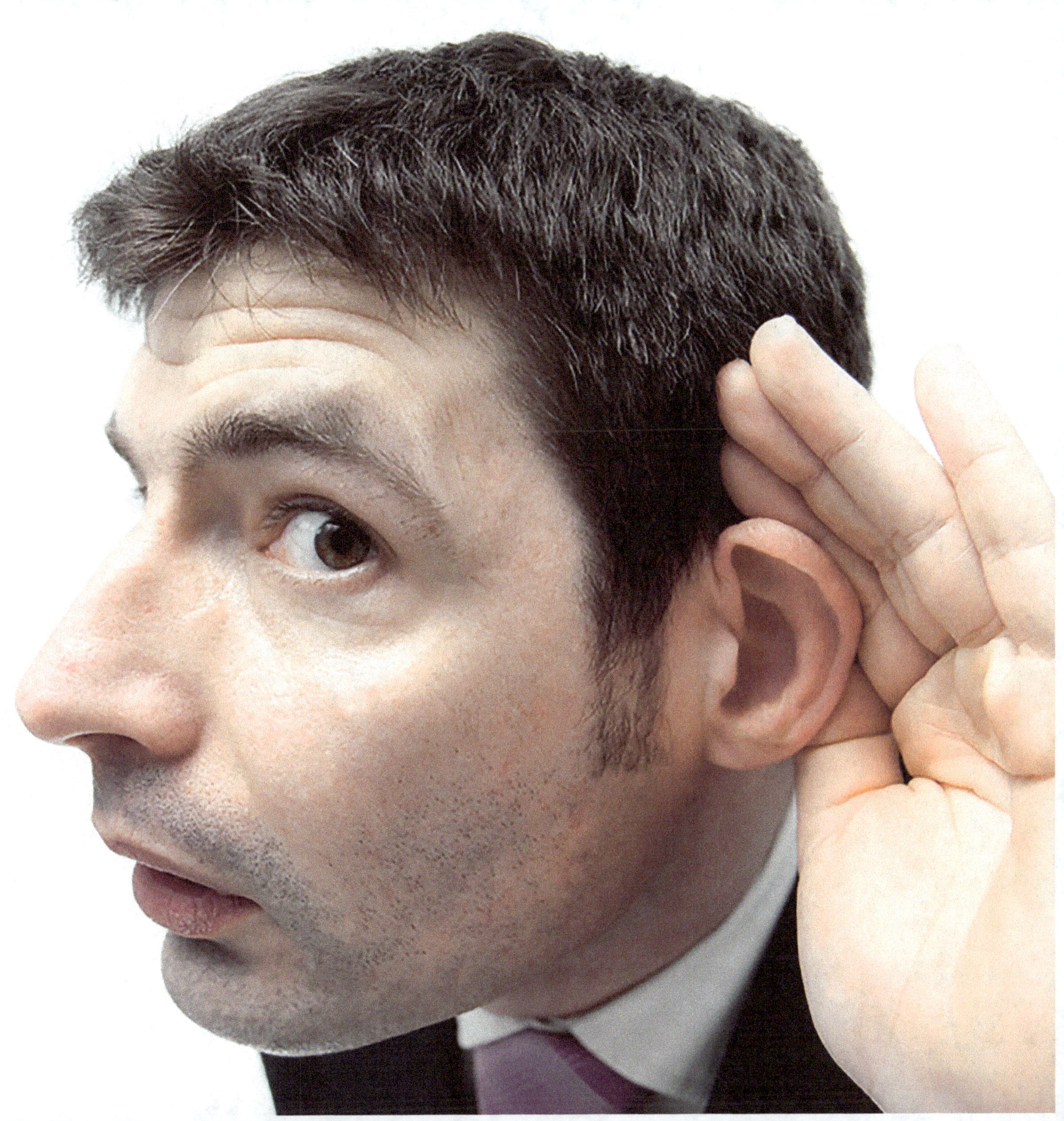

WHY DO WE HAVE TWO EARS?

We have two ears to help determine the sound's direction. Our brains are intelligent enough to know that if it reaches one ear just prior to reaching the other and is a little bit louder, then it knows the direction from which it came from. We also have ears on both sides of our head to help hear better.

WHY AM I DIZZY?

There are many signals that our brain takes in from our body to maintain balance. The fluid located in the inner ear is one of them. How the fluid is moving tells your brain a lot.

Our eyes and sense of touch are also used by our brain to maintain position and balance. If you spin around really fast and then come to an abrupt stop, the fluid keeps spinning, but your body and your eyes have stopped. This is what causes your brain to become confused for a short time and make you feel dizzy.

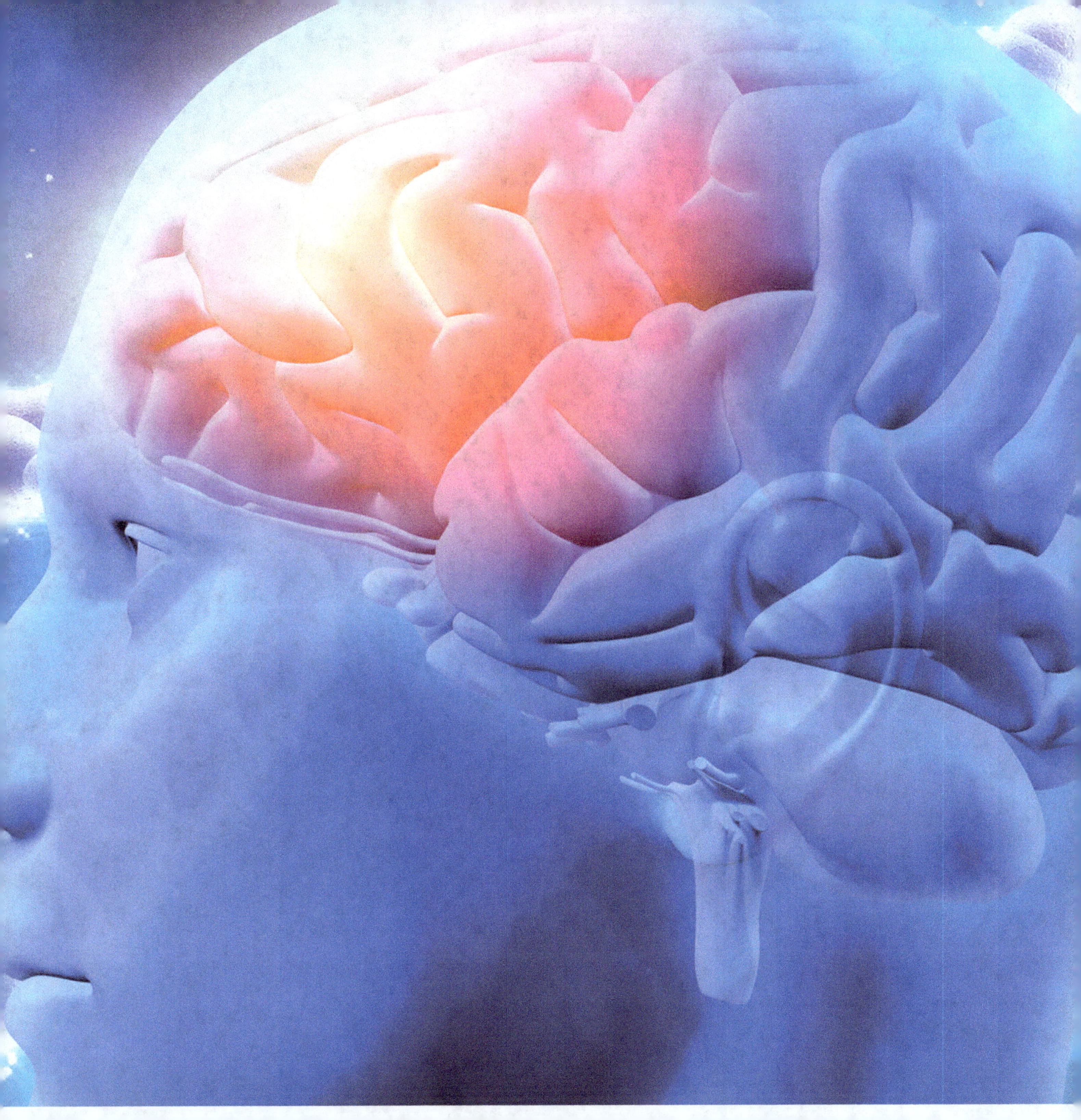

JBL

WHAT IS SOUND?

A wave, or vibration, that is able to travel through matter (gas, liquid, or solid) and can be heard is sound.

HOW IS IT ABLE TO MOVE?

A vibration starts by some type of mechanical movement, like someone knocking on a door or plucking a guitar string. It then creates a vibration next to the event's molecules (like your hand striking the door when you knock on it).

PLAYING A GUITAR

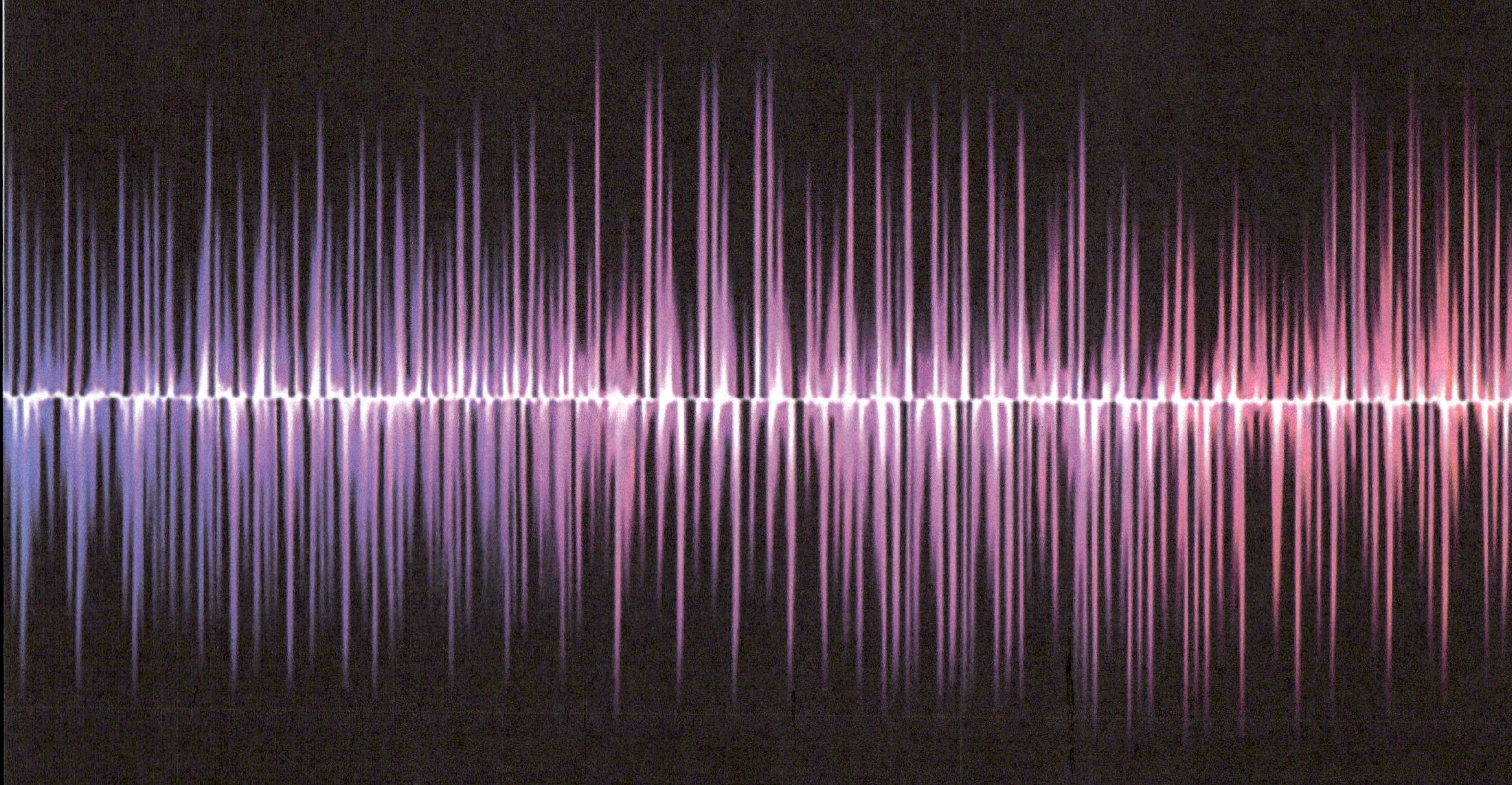

As these particular molecules begin to vibrate, they cause the surrounding molecules to vibrate. This vibration then spreads from one molecule to another which causes it to travel.

It has to travel through matter since it requires vibration of the molecules to propagate. The matter transporting it is known as its medium.

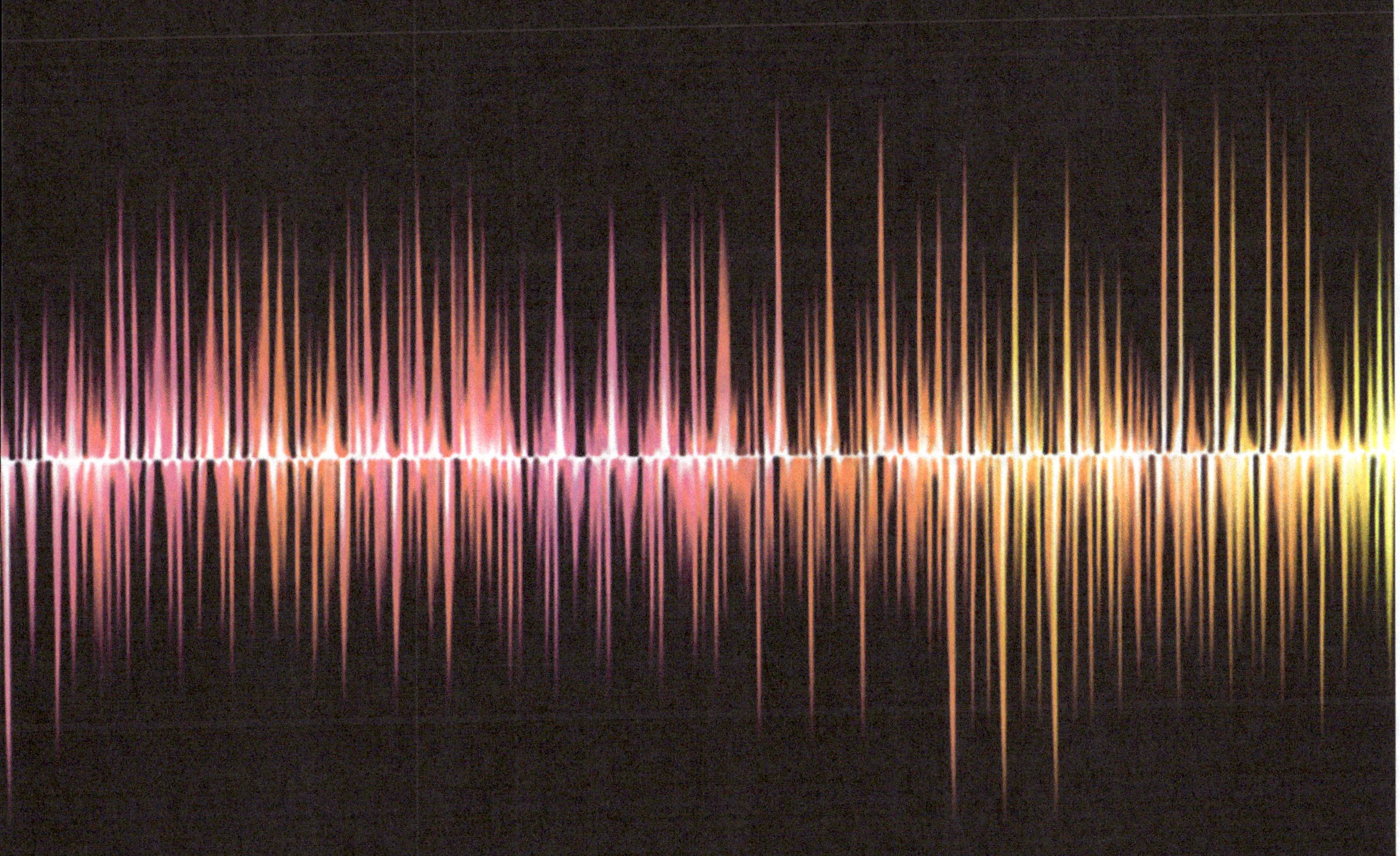

WHAT IS THE SPEED OF SOUND

How fast a wave or vibration passes through its medium is the speed of sound. The type of medium will have a great impact on how quickly sound can pass through it. It will travel quicker through water than air, and even quicker through steel.

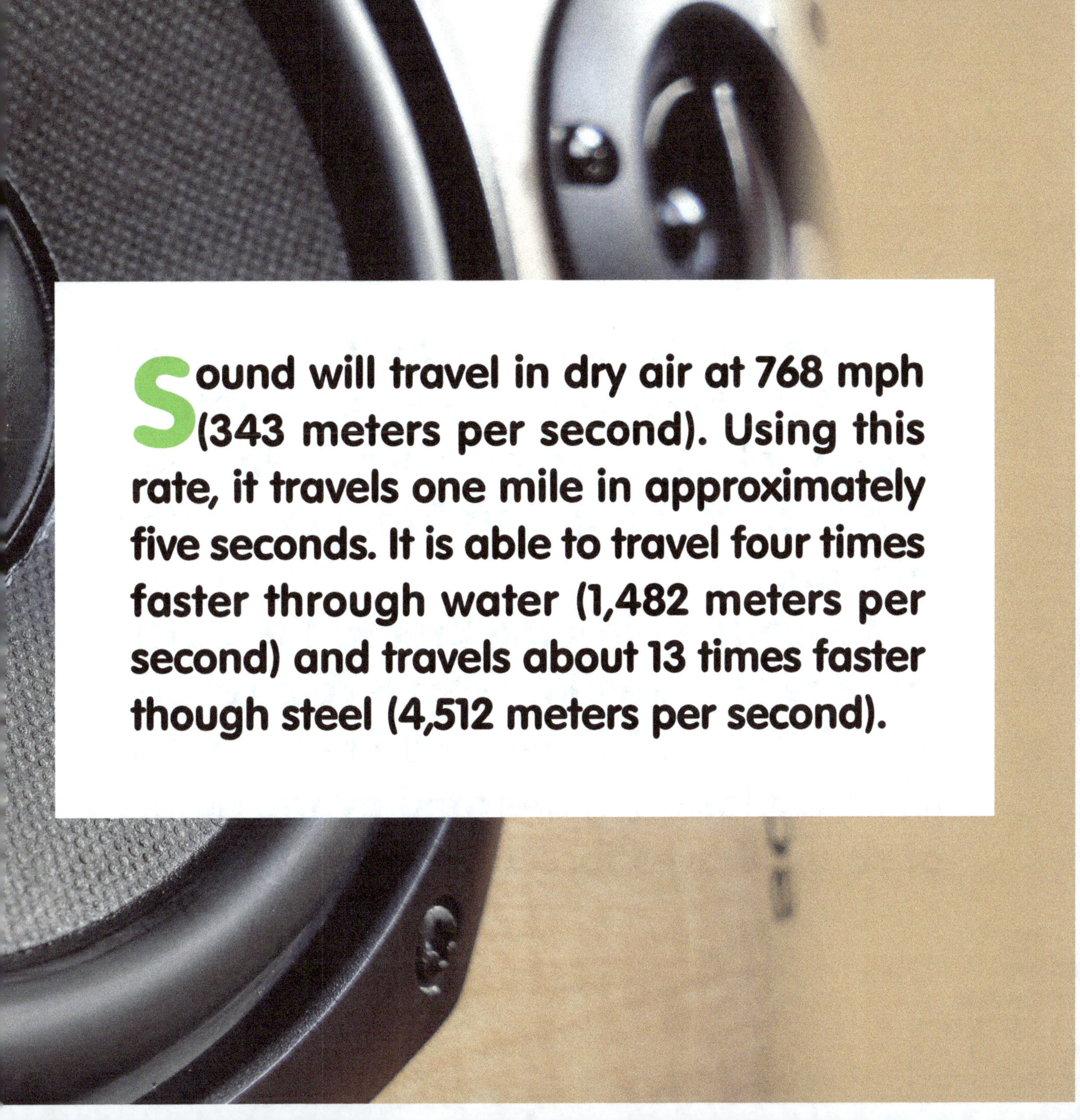

Sound will travel in dry air at 768 mph (343 meters per second). Using this rate, it travels one mile in approximately five seconds. It is able to travel four times faster through water (1,482 meters per second) and travels about 13 times faster though steel (4,512 meters per second).

THE SOUND BARRIER

When an airplane is able to travel faster than the speed of sound, it is referred to as breaking the sound barrier. While most airplanes do not go this fast, many fighter jets can.

When the airplane breaks the barrier, they are also creating what is referred to as a sonic boom. This is a loud noise, similar to an explosion, generated by the amount of sound waves forced together.

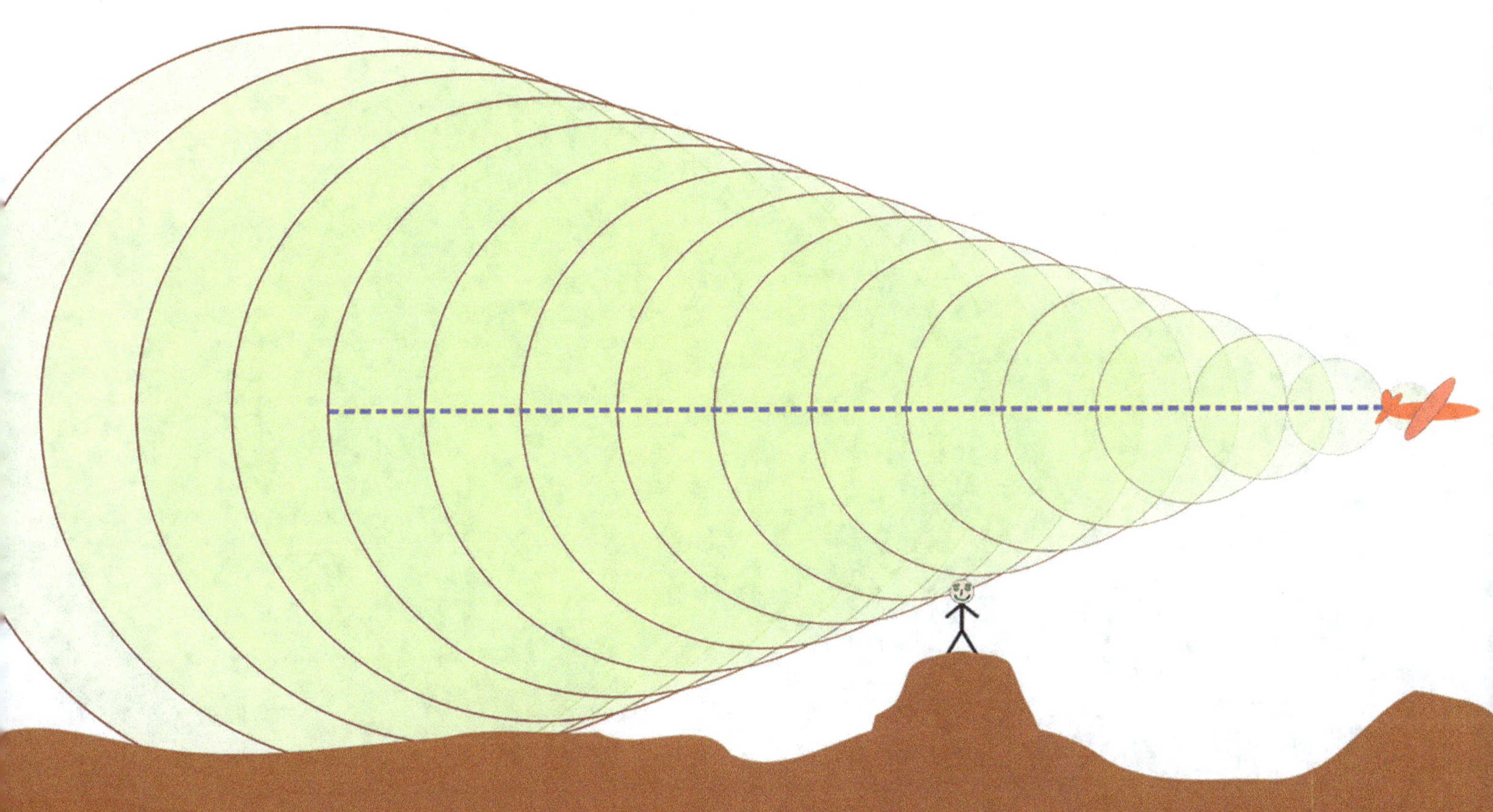

SONIC BOOM

VOLUME
min
VOLUME CONTROLLER

VOLUME

The sound volume measure's the loudness. We use decibels to quantify the volume. The louder it is, the higher the number of decibels. A slight sound, similar to a whisper, measures approximately 15-20 decibels. A louder sound, similar to that of a jet engine, is about 150 decibels. The pain threshold is about 130 decibels.

Loud sounds can damage your ears, causing a loss of hearing ability. Sound at 85 decibels can damage your ears if listened to over a long time period. This is why it is not good to listen to loud music and have your headphones up too loud.

EAR CHECK UP

AUDIO FREQUENCY

FREQUENCY AND PITCH

One of the more important measurements of sound is its frequency, which is the speed that the wave is oscillating, which differs from the speed that the wave travels through a medium. Hertz is how we measure frequency.

The faster the wave oscillates, the higher its pitch will be. An example would a guitar, the large heavier string vibrates slower and creates a low pitch or sound. The thinner, lighter string vibrates faster and creates a higher pitch or sound.

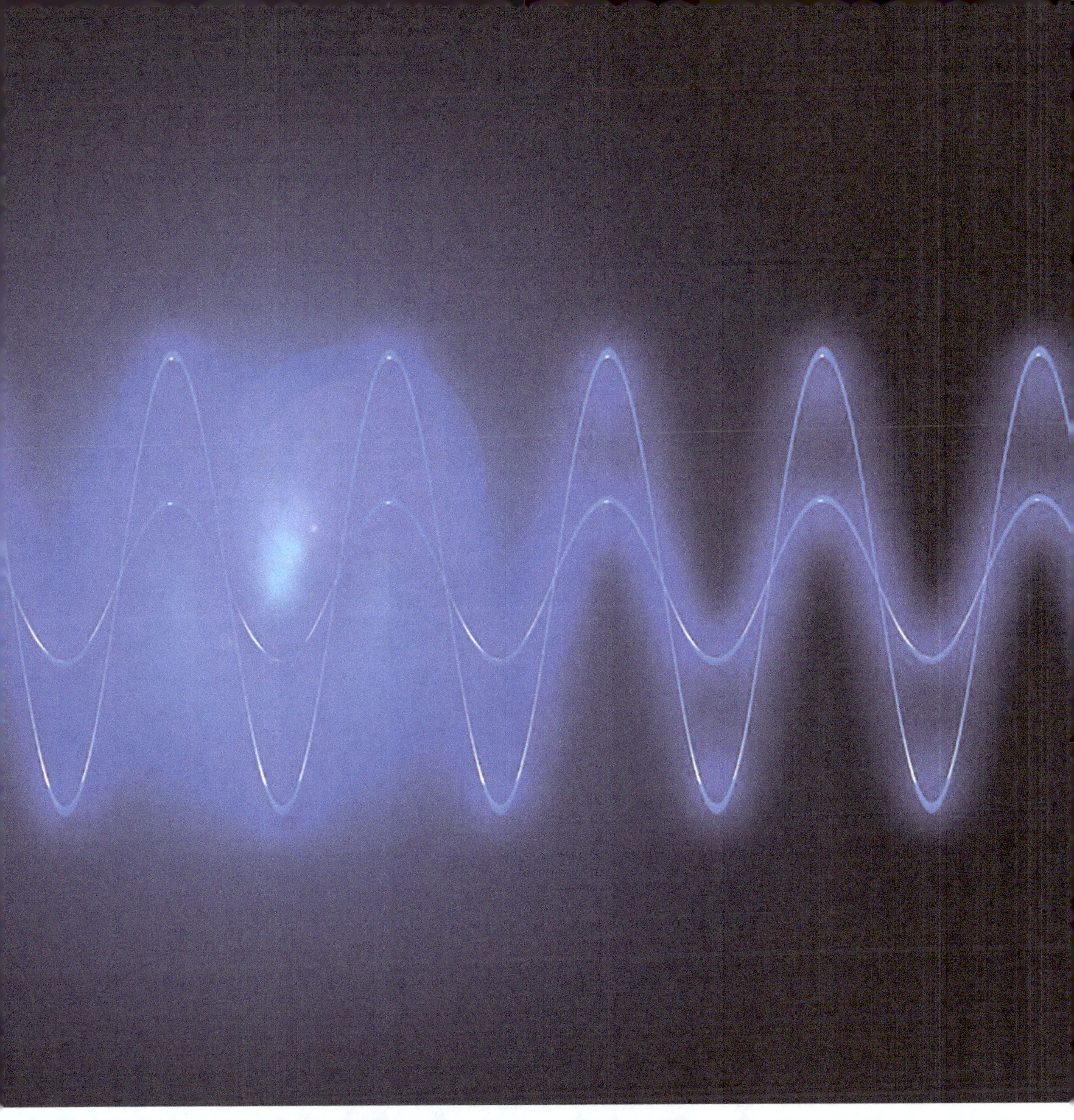

We are able to hear a sound within a frequency range of approximately 20 Hz on the lower end, and 20,000 Hz on the higher end. Many animals have different frequency ranges.

One example is the dolphin, they cannot hear sounds as low as we are able to, but they can hear higher sounds over 100,000 Hz. Cats and dogs are able to hear higher pitched sounds that humans are. Have you ever heard of a dog whistle? The dog can hear the whistle, but we cannot.

COMMUNICATION THROUGH TALKING

WHAT ABOUT TALKING?

In addition to the importance of hearing sound, it is also used for communication. The process used to make precise sounds is quite complex and utilizes many body parts working with each other. The vibration of the vocal cords in your throat is how sounds are created.

We use our lungs to force the air to move past our vocal cords to start the vibration. Our mouths and tongues are used for forming specific sounds. It is quite a complex system we use in creating communication. Think about this process and how amazing it is the next time you are talking.

CONCERT HALL

ACOUSTICS

The study of the travel of sound is known as acoustics. It is significant to control how it reacts and is used in the design of buildings such as libraries, theaters and auditoriums. Occasionally, acoustics is utilized in helping sound to travel. A good example is in a big concert hall, acoustics helps everyone in the building to hear the music, including those in the back seats. The acoustic design in a library helps in keeping it from traveling to keep it quiet.

TWO WAYS TO CONTROL ACOUSTICS:

Reverberation is how sound bounces off of things. A "loud" room typically might be a room where it reverberates off the floors and walls. Certain materials echo sounds better than others do. A tile floor reverberates sound better than a carpeted floor does since the carpet absorbs the sound.

MUSIC ROOM

Absorption is the opposite of reverberation, and items absorbing the sound do not reflect vibrations. Softer items like curtains and carpet help absorb sound and keep the room quieter.

WHAT IS THE DOPPLER EFFECT?

As you stand still while a car goes past you, the sound's frequency changes while the car moves past you. This is referred to as the Doppler Effect. As the car comes towards you, the sound pitch is higher and then as the car moves away from you, the pitch gets lower.

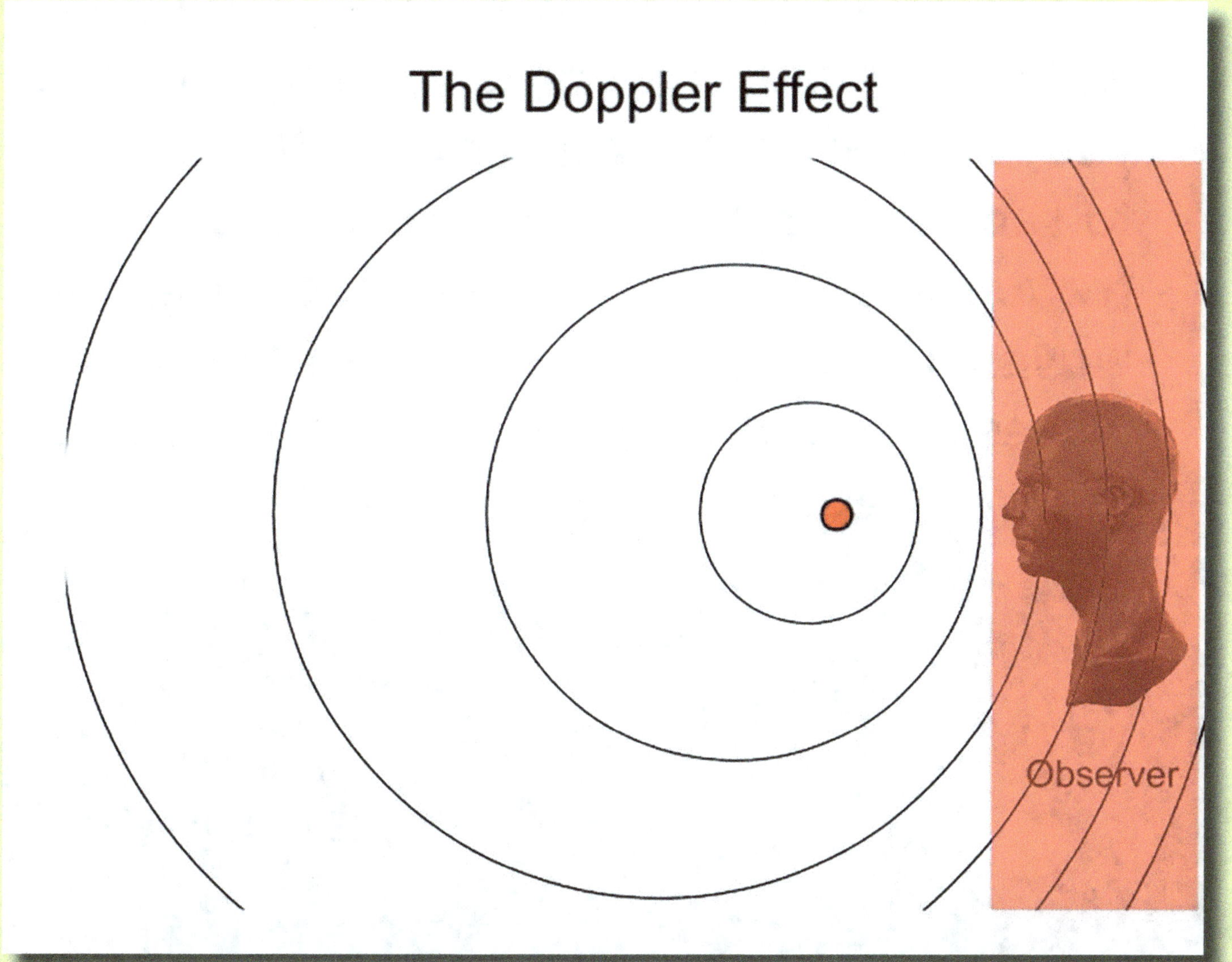

The Doppler Effect

The sound produced by the car does not change, nor does the frequency. However, when the car is coming towards you, its speed is what causes the waves to reach your ear sooner, or at a greater frequency, than the car is producing the waves. Once the car has passed you, the waves of sound actually reach your ears at a lower frequency.

THE DOPPLER EFFECT WAS NAMED FOR
CHRISTIAN DOPPLER, THE SCIENTIST
WHO DISCOVERED THIS IN 1842.

Now that you have learned how our ears work and the basics of sound, think about what happens whenever you listen to music, have a conversation or scream at someone. For additional information about our ears and how sound works you can go to your local library, research the internet, or ask questions of your teachers, family, and friends.

Visit
BABY PROFESSOR
EDUCATION KIDS
www.BabyProfessorBooks.com
to download Free Baby Professor eBooks
and view our catalog of new and exciting
Children's Books